The Urbana Free Library

To renew materials call
217-367-4057

History of American Immigration

PETER A. HAMMERSCHMIDT

MAJOR AMERICAN IMMIGRATION

MASON CREST PUBLISHERS • PHILADELPHIA

A group of immigrants cheer and wave their hats as they catch their first glimpse of the Statue of Liberty. For many, this dramatic view of New York Harbor on the way to Ellis Island was their introduction to America.

History of American Immigration

PETER A. HAMMERSCHMIDT

MAJOR AMERICAN IMMIGRATION

MASON CREST PUBLISHERS • PHILADELPHIA

3/10
23⁰⁰

Mason Crest Publishers
370 Reed Road
Broomall PA 19008
www.masoncrest.com

Copyright © 2009 by Mason Crest Publishers. All rights reserved.
Printed and bound in Malaysia.

First printing

1 3 5 7 9 8 6 4 2

Library of Congress Cataloging-in-Publication Data

Hammerschmidt, Peter A., 1973-
  History of American immigration / Peter A. Hammerschmidt.
     p. cm. — (Major American immigration)
  Includes index.
  ISBN 978-1-4222-0613-3 (hardcover)
  ISBN 978-1-4222-0680-5 (pbk.)
  1. United States—Emigration and immigration—History—
Juvenile literature. I. Title.
  JV6450.M666 2008
  304.8'73009—dc22
                                        2008028222

Table of Contents

MAJOR AMERICAN IMMIGRATION

America's Ethnic Heritage

Barry Moreno, librarian
Statue of Liberty/
Ellis Island National Monument

Ethnic diversity is one of the most striking characteristics of the American identity. In the United States the Bureau of the Census officially recognizes 122 different ethnic groups. North America's population had grown by leaps and bounds, starting with the American Indian tribes and nations—the continent's original people—and increasing with the arrival of the European colonial migrants who came to these shores during the 16th and 17th centuries. Since then, millions of immigrants have come to America from every corner of the world.

But the passage of generations and the great distance of America from the "Old World"—Europe, Africa, and Asia—has in some cases separated immigrant peoples from their roots. The struggle to succeed in America made it easy to forget past traditions. Further, the American spirit of freedom, individualism, and equality gave Americans a perspective quite different from the view of life shared by residents of the Old World.

Immigrants of the 19th and 20th centuries recognized this at once. Many tried to "Americanize" themselves by tossing away their peasant clothes and dressing American-style even before reaching their new homes in the cities or the countryside of America. It was not so easy to become part of America's culture, however. For many immigrants, learning English was quite a hurdle. In fact, most older immigrants clung to the old ways, preferring to speak their native languages and follow their familiar customs and traditions. This was easy to do when ethnic neighborhoods abounded in large North American cities like New York, Montreal, Philadelphia, Chicago, Toronto, Boston, Cleveland, St. Louis, New Orleans and San Francisco. In rural areas, farm families—many of them Scandinavian, German, or Czech—established their own tightly knit communities. Thus foreign languages and dialects, religious beliefs, Old World customs, and certain class distinctions flourished.

The most striking changes occurred among the children of immigrants, whose hopes and dreams were different from those of their parents. They began breaking away from the Old World customs, perhaps as a reaction to the embarrassment of being labeled "foreigner." They badly wanted to be Americans, and assimilated more easily than their parents and grandparents. They learned to speak English without a foreign accent, to dress and act like other Americans. The assimilation of the children of immigrants was encouraged by social contact—games, schools, jobs, and military service—which further broke down the barriers between immigrant groups and hastened the process of Americanization. Along the way, many family traditions were lost or abandoned.

Today, the pride that Americans have in their ethnic roots is one of the abiding strengths of both the United States and Canada. It shows that the theory which called America a "melting pot" of the world's people was never really true. The thought that a single "American" would emerge from the combination of these peoples has never happened, for Americans have grown more reluctant than ever before to forget the struggles of their ethnic forefathers. The growth of cultural studies and genealogical research indicates that Americans are anxious not to entirely lose this identity, whether it is English, French, Chinese, African, Mexican, or some other group. There is an interest in tracing back the family line as far as records or memory will take them. In a sense, this has made Americans a divided people; proud to be Americans, but proud also of their ethnic roots.

As a result, many Americans have welcomed a new identity, that of the hyphenated American. This unique description has grown in usage over the years and continues to grow as more Americans recognize the importance of family heritage. In the end, this is an appreciation of America's great cultural heritage and its richness of its variety.

The Statue of Liberty overlooks New York Harbor. Since 1886, it has been a symbol for millions of immigrants who hoped to start a new life in America.

The Promise of Lady Liberty

The awesome sight of Lady Liberty towering over New York Harbor has welcomed immigrants into the United States for more than 100 years. Not only did she signal the end of a long and exhausting journey for the newcomers; she also held the promise of freedom, limitless opportunity, and a new and better life.

As each ship filled with immigrants made its way into the harbor, hundreds of men, women, and children would hang off the ship's railings, amazed by the colossal statue. Her torch was like a beacon, calling out to the masses seeking shelter in America. Her crown of seven spikes represented freedom—shining out to each of the world's seven continents and seven seas. And the chains lying broken at her feet signified the overthrow of **oppression**.

Under her feet and flowing robes, inscribed in bronze on the statue's base, are the following words:

> *Give me your tired, your poor,*
> *Your huddled masses yearning to breathe free,*
> *The wretched refuse of your teeming shore.*
> *Send these, the homeless, tempest-tost to me.*
> *I lift my lamp beside the golden door!*

It was on the promise of these words that the "huddled masses" came—came by the tens of millions.

The settlement of North America is one of the great stories of modern history. Ever since the early days of **colonization**, immigrants crossed every ocean to reach the United States and Canada. Children, parents, and grandparents of all **ethnic groups** flocked to the New World. They came to flee religious or political **persecution** and to escape starvation or a life of hardship and suffering. Most of all, they came to find work and seek riches. To each of them, North America was seen as a place of great opportunity and freedom.

Immigration had an especially big impact on American history. Without the energy and labor of its immigrants, the United States would not have become the world power it is today. The newcomers arrived as laborers, farmers, businessmen, or shop owners. They dug the canals, cut the timber, mined the coal, ran the factories, opened the stores, herded the cattle, laid the railroad tracks, and plowed the uncut prairies. Together, these pioneers and businesspeople expanded and settled a wild continent.

What also made immigration to America so special was the sheer scale. Until the 1900s, immigration to the United States was relatively easy. Between 1820 (when immigration record-keeping first began) and 2008, some 70 million people came to the United States. An additional five million arrived further north on Canada's shores.

Today, the United States and Canada are more diverse than any other countries in the world. The traditions, beliefs, and values of hundreds of ethnic groups have come together to create a cultural **mosaic** that is constantly changing. This is because immigrants don't

Passengers cheer as their ship approaches the Statue of Liberty. For many immigrants, the sight of the famous landmark meant the most difficult part of their journey was over.

just bring their belongings across the oceans—they also bring their cultures, traditions, languages, and dreams. Their gifts to North America include science, music, politics, inventions, painting, literature, movies, food, and technology. All together, the influence of immigrants gives American society a richness and variety that is truly unique.

Immigrant passengers prepare to disembark as their ship arrives at Ellis Island. They still faced tests and doctor's examinations that could mean the difference between staying in America and being sent back to their country of origin.

The history of immigration to America is not without its rough periods, however. Differences between people have often created tensions. The waves of people flooding the country washed the tragedy of slavery onto America's shores. The thrust of settlement upset the world of the Native Americans. And at various times, rules designed to keep immigrants out—rather than welcome them in—were created by lawmakers trying to "protect" society.

Despite these differences, however, all Americans today share in their country's diversity. America's multicultural society means that all people can keep their individual identities and take pride in where they are from. It also means that each of them can fulfill the promise of Lady Liberty—a life of freedom and opportunity in a new country. ✹

The arrival of Christopher Columbus in the New World led to centuries of European exploration and settlement of North and South America.

2 The First Arrivals

Immigration to North America began long before the arrival of Christopher Columbus in 1492. Evidence suggests that Viking explorers spent several years in Newfoundland shortly after A.D. 1000. And, of course, Native Americans had settled large parts of the land before any of the European visitors. It was the arrival of Columbus, however, that truly opened the New World to Europe and sparked the great age of exploration and expansion in North America.

The Spaniards were the first to arrive. In 1513, Juan Ponce de Léon of Spain discovered and named Florida. A few years after conquering the ancient Aztec civilization in Mexico, Hernán Cortés sent voyages to explore California, and from 1540 to 1542 Francisco Coronado explored the American Southwest.

The French followed, concentrating most of their exploration further north in Atlantic Canada and Quebec. By 1541, Jacques Cartier had explored much of the St. Lawrence River basin and penetrated the interior as far as modern Montreal. Another great French explorer, Samuel de Champlain, arrived in 1603 and moved into Acadia and Canada itself. By 1608, Champlain had established a permanent colony in what is now Quebec City.

Seeing the strong Spanish and French interest in the New World, the English also began sailing across the Atlantic before it was too late and all the land had been claimed. They experienced mild success in the early years. Though John Cabot had discovered rich fishing grounds off the coast of Labrador in 1497, attempts at colonization in the Carolinas by Sir Walter Raleigh failed. It was not until the 1607 landing at Jamestown, Virginia—named after King James I—that the English were able to establish a permanent American foothold.

The ultimate origins of the American people can be traced back to this arrival. Soon after the English showed that permanent colonies could survive in the New World, large-scale immigration to America began.

The remains of a Spanish fort in St. Augustine, Florida. In 1565, the Spanish established St. Augustine. The city is the oldest continuous European settlement in North America.

Settlers trade with Indians in Jamestown, the first permanent English settlement in America. While some settlers tried to keep peaceful relations with the Native Americans, peace would be hard to maintain.

Among America's first immigrants were those seeking freedom from religious persecution. In September 1620, over 100 English religious separatists calling themselves Pilgrims set out on a four-month sea voyage to America. On December 11, their small ship the *Mayflower* sailed into the harbor at Plymouth in what later became Massachusetts. Upon their arrival, the Pilgrims quickly established the roots of the greatest of American traditions—a system of democratic self-government.

Soon after the Pilgrim landing, the great ***convoys*** of immigrants pursuing the "American adventure" began to arrive. Throughout the 1630s (a period known as the "Great Migration"), 200 ships transported 20,000 Englishmen and women to New England. Many more immigrants followed, joining their countrymen in settlements at Virginia, Maryland, New Hampshire, Connecticut, Rhode Island, and New York. Immigrants from the rest of Europe came as well—from Germany, Holland, Switzerland, Sweden, and even Finland.

By 1660, however, the rate of immigration began to slow. The British government was worried that too many of its citizens would leave for America, and officially discouraged immigration to the New World. During the 1700s, Britain began to actually restrict immigration to its North American colonies. In 1718, the British Parliament prohibited all skilled workers from migrating. British immigration to the colonies was completely halted when revolutionary violence broke out in 1775, and did not begin again until 1814. Many American colonists who supported the British during the American Revolution chose to **emigrate** to Canada during this time.

Other European nations quickly made up for the decrease in British immigration. In the early part of the 18th century, many residents of

English colonies in North America attracted many people who wanted to escape religious persecution during the mid-17th century— a time when England was embroiled in civil war.

PENNSYLVANIA

The settlement of Pennsylvania was typical of the American immigration experience. William Penn, a Quaker who suffered persecution in England for his religious beliefs, established a colony in 1682 based on the principles of religious and political freedom. Penn opened the door wide to anyone who wished to live there. It took 23 ships to transport his first group of immigrants, and plenty more soon followed.

In addition to the Swedes, Dutch, and English already living in North America, Penn brought people into his colony from Barbados, Jamaica, Scotland, and Ireland. Immigrants from Wales also came, forming a separate, Welsh-speaking area that kept its culture for generations. Germans in particular were attracted to Penn's colony. Pennsylvania became such a favored destination for German immigration that between 1682 and the 1750s, over 100,000 Germans settled there.

As in many other parts of America, the sheer bounty of Pennsylvania was the main attraction. With its rich soil and fertile valleys, this was "the best poor man's country," where immigrant farmers could thrive.

Ireland left for America because of high rents and *famines*. By the 1760s, they were joined by Scottish *artisans* and laborers, many of whom moved to the tobacco colonies to work on the *plantations*. From 1720 to 1770, about half a million men, women, and children from

African-American slaves harvest sugar cane on an American plantation. During the colonial period, slaves could be found in every North American colony.

northern Ireland and Scotland emigrated to Pennsylvania. Tens of thousands of Germans also came in the early 1700s, escaping the wars of Europe or seeking religious freedom.

Immigration to colonial America was encouraged because of the need for cheap labor to build the growing country. Craftsmen, timber mills, and plantation farmers needed more and more settlers and workers to expand their businesses. A system of *indentured service* was introduced to the colonies to fulfill this need. It is estimated that over half of all the white laborers drawn to the colonies before 1776 were indentured servants. They were generally poor English people who worked in the colonies for a number of years to pay off their debts and gain their freedom. Many of these indentured servants either died because of bad living conditions or completed their service and left their employers. Thus, the need for new labor was constant.

To meet this demand, Virginian planters turned to African labor. In 1619, the first African slave laborers arrived by ship and were sold to plantations in Virginia, South Carolina, and Maryland. As black slaves replaced white indentured laborers, the plantations became even more dependent on slave labor. By the time of American independence in 1776, there were hundreds of thousands of these "involuntary immigrants" in the colonies. ✸

A wagon train of hopeful settlers departs for land in Oregon and the West. As the states along the Atlantic coast became more crowded, many of the immigrants who came to America headed west, where land was available on the frontier.

3 The Great Rush to Prosperity

Why did so many immigrants come to America? Why did millions of families uproot their lives and move so far across the world to a foreign land? The biggest attraction was the simple promise of a good, honest, and fulfilling life.

Right before he died, Benjamin Franklin wrote a pamphlet giving advice to Europeans planning to come to America. In it, he said that his country was a good place for those who wanted to become rich. But he also said that America was a haven for the hard-working poor as well. He wrote that "nowhere else are the laboring poor so well fed, well lodged, well clothed, and well paid as in the United States of America."

Franklin's promise of a simple but successful life brought many people across the Atlantic Ocean. Artisans and laborers forced out of work in Europe were amazed at how easy it was to find jobs in North America. Because wood was everywhere, English carpenters and furniture makers were soon kept busy. Italians and Poles ran the first glass factories in America, and many Dutch immigrants made pottery or worked as portrait painters.

Cheap and plentiful land also played a role in bringing immigrants over. In the early days of the new colonies, many immigrants simply settled on open land and began farming. Even after the 1796 Land

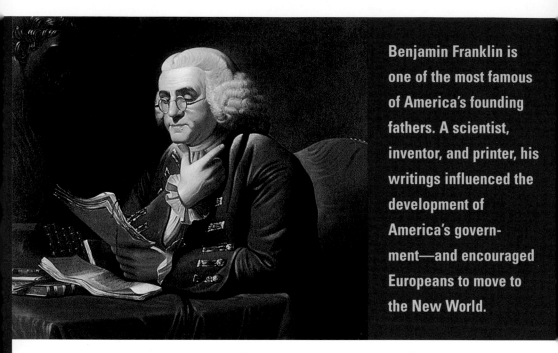

Benjamin Franklin is one of the most famous of America's founding fathers. A scientist, inventor, and printer, his writings influenced the development of America's govern- ment—and encouraged Europeans to move to the New World.

Purchase Act, land cost only $2 an acre if you bought at least 320 acres. Even better, the buyer only had to pay 25 percent of the cost immediately and could pay the rest over four years. This meant that any immigrant family could buy a big farm—an enormous one by European standards—for only $160 cash. And the further south one moved, the cheaper land got. By snapping up this inexpensive land, immigrants quickly populated the areas of what are now North Carolina, Kentucky, Tennessee, and Georgia.

What was on the land was just as important as the price. European immigrants soon found that many crops could be grown in North American soil with great success. Crops like corn produced twice as much food per acre as traditional English crops. Europeans were also amazed by the huge variety of food that was available. Many had never before tasted foods such as turkey, wild plums, cherries, pumpkins, squash, beans, melons, blackberries, and strawberries.

The variety and amount of wildlife was staggering to the Europeans. Big game, such as deer and buffalo, were excellent sources of meat, and fish and seafood were abundant. Smaller creatures, such as the weasel, badger, mink, and beaver, helped generate a lucrative fur trade, especially in Canada.

Though these natural resources provided an excellent quality of life, the sheer quantity of wood was the greatest gift. Already by the early 1600s, wood in Western Europe was increasingly scarce and expensive. Ordinary European families could never get enough. In North America, by contrast, cheap wood was everywhere, so the colonists always had enough wood to build their houses and to burn for warmth.

Many other things about North America were attractive. There were no church taxes because there was no state church. State taxation was low, so workers were able to keep most of their wages to spend on their families. Europeans, who suffered under heavy taxation, could not believe their ears when they heard that an American farm with eight horses paid only $12 a year in tax. Wage rates were also much higher than in Europe.

The lack of social or political oppression was also important. There was no military **conscription** or political police. There were no legalized class distinctions, as was the case in Europe. Except for slaves, no one called anyone "Master," and anyone, if they were willing to work for it, could become part of the upper class. In most cases, employers would eat at the same table as their employees.

New immigrants spread the news of these blessings back to the Old World. Letters speaking of the good life were mailed back home and read aloud to entire villages. These accounts were also used as recruitment *propaganda* for the transatlantic shipping companies, which made huge amounts of money carrying new immigrants to the United States.

Becoming an American was easy in the early 1800s. An Englishman, without luggage, a passport, or health certificate, could pay a small amount of money to a shipping company in Liverpool and go to sea. Once the ship reached New York, he could walk ashore without any authorities asking him his business and then just become a part of the new society. Sometimes, it was not even necessary to have the money. Travel to Canada was provided free for British citizens. Upon arriving in Canada, many would find rides on coastal boats to New York or Massachusetts. About 100,000 people arrived in America between 1815 and 1820 without having to show any sort of identification.

With travel so easy and the chance of success so high, immigration exploded during the 1800s. Pressures in Europe were also responsible for pushing immigrants to North American shores. The Old World was becoming crowded—in only 150 years, Europe's population grew by 250 million people. This produced a huge outflow of immigrants, most

Many newcomers to America moved west, where they could purchase land cheaply. These immigrants often built modest cabins and established small farms.

of whom went to the United States.

Food shortages were another factor. The bad weather of 1816—Europe's "year without a summer"—and the brutal winters of 1825, 1826, and 1829 caused severe hunger and famines. A potato famine and generally poor conditions drove at least 20 percent of Ireland's entire population to other shores between 1844 and 1854; most came to the United States and Canada.

From 1815 to the start of the Civil War, over five million people left Europe for the United States. More than 70 percent came from England or Ireland; the rest came from other European countries. Though the Civil War (1861–1865) stopped most immigration, the arrival of new Americans resumed on an even larger scale after the war ended. Over the next 25 years, another 10 million reached America's shores.

Until 1890, most immigrants came from England, Ireland, Wales, and Germany. Soon, however, the ethnic makeup of new arrivals began to change. Many of the 15 million immigrants who came to America between 1890 and the start of World War I in 1914 were from eastern and southern Europe. This new rush of immigration included Poles, Ukrainians, Slovaks, Croatians, Hungarians, Greeks, Romanians, and Italians. Thousands of Jews also came, fleeing the *pogroms* taking place in eastern Europe and the Russian Empire.

An immigrant homesteader turns over the sod on his Montana farm, circa 1908.

A NEW LAND, A NEW IDENTITY

Many southern and eastern European immigrants changed much more than just their nationality upon arrival in America. To help them adjust to their new country (and to help Americans adjust to them), many changed their names. Most welcomed this change. Immigrants found that an *Anglicized* name gave them better chances at job interviews and that their children would have less trouble at school.

Most often, their new names were simply changed to sound more "American." First names like Rolf became Ralph, Margit became Margaret, Davnar became David, and Benedetto became Benny. Last names were often shortened or made to sound more Christian: Fogelman became Fogg and Wallik became Wallace. Since a great number of immigrants came to America as children, many of their names were Anglicized when they registered at public school.

Names were not the only part of an immigrant's identity that could change. Because some immigrants left their birth certificates behind, lost them during their journey over, or came from areas where birth records were not kept, they didn't even know their own birthdays. Many had to make up new birthdays when filling out paperwork in the United States.

Those from the first waves of immigration turned primarily to farming when they arrived in the United States, helping to expand the country westward. To populate its barren frontiers, the government provided immigrants with cheap, or even free, land. The Homestead Act of 1862 gave away 160 acres of public land to anyone who claimed it and lived on it for five years. Under this law, Midwestern states such as Minnesota, Wisconsin, Illinois, and the Dakotas became home to thousands of Germans, Swedish, Norwegians, and other northern European immigrants during the mid-1800s.

Canada also used cheap land to attract settlers. The Canadian West, which was enormous but thinly populated, was opened up to immigrants in 1872 with the Dominion Lands Act. Any settler over 21 years old who paid a $10 registration fee could receive 160 acres of land to live on and cultivate. With this plan, the Canadian government brought Russians, Ukrainians, Hungarians, and even Icelanders to their open prairies.

The huge railroad projects in the American West were a magnet for those seeking work. Immigrants swarmed in from poor villages in China, from famine-stricken Ireland, and from England, France, and Germany to lay thousands of miles of track. They endured horrible conditions—months of living in tents, blasting away at the land, carrying iron rails, and driving spikes into the ground. Canada's Pacific Railway, built through the steep and winding Rocky Mountains, also brought in thousands of immigrants. Hundreds of men lost their lives to disease and injury while laying the tracks.

Rather than brave the frontier, many other new immigrants flocked to America's growing industrial cities. Southern and eastern Europeans went wherever there was a demand for unskilled labor. They usually ended up working in loud, dirty, and dangerous factories. Jews, Slavs, Italians, Romanians, and Greeks soon became concentrated in cities

Immigrant laborers—particularly Chinese and Irish—helped to build the transcontinental railroad.

like New York, Chicago, Cleveland, Detroit, and Boston, where industry was booming.

Even though American cities were exploding in size in the early 1900s and the demand for labor was still strong, World War I brought the second great wave of American immigration to an end. In 1914, 1.2 million immigrants reached American shores. By 1918, however, only 100,000 were arriving each year. This was only a temporary slowdown, however, for once the war ended, Lady Liberty reopened her golden door. ☀

Ellis Island has been restored, and today is a museum of immigration history. Ferries take visitors to the island, where they can learn about the experiences of immigrants.

4 Island of Hope, Island of Tears

No name is as closely linked to American immigration as Ellis Island. From its opening in 1892 to its closure in 1954, this facility in New York Harbor witnessed the largest wave of human **migration** in modern history. Under Lady Liberty's gaze, more than 12 million immigrants were processed at Ellis Island and admitted into American society. Today, over 100 million Americans can trace their roots back to an ancestor who entered the country through Ellis Island.

The journey would begin far from New York's shores. In the early 1900s, crossing the Atlantic by steamship could take anywhere from six to eight days. Though this was a long trip, it was still far better than the weeks or months it took the wind-powered ships of the 1700s. Since most immigrants were poor to start with, many were unable to afford the more expensive tickets and traveled in **steerage**.

The conditions left much to be desired: the ships were crowded, damp, smelly, and had poor ventilation. Since there was nothing but cold water (and no showers or baths), washing was a luxury. Toilets didn't function well, and the facilities were poorly kept. To make matters worse, travelers suffering from seasickness during bad weather could not get onto the deck to "get sick" over the ship's rails. With these overcrowded and unsanitary conditions, as well as a frequent lack of food, illness was common. Some immigrants did not survive the journey.

Immigrants walk up the path to the main building at Ellis Island, circa 1900. From 1892 to 1954, Ellis Island was the main entry station for people wishing to come to America.

For the immigrants who survived the journey, however, the ordeal was worth it. As they steamed into New York and caught a glimpse of the Statue of Liberty, they knew their journey was over and their freedom only steps away.

But the trip was not over yet. After docking, the first- and second-class passengers were let off. Since they had money, most were processed through Customs quickly. The third- and fourth-class passengers in steerage, however, were crammed onto ferries or barges and brought to the immigration processing station. Once there, they would deposit all their belongings in the main building and begin the final part of their ordeal: the medical and legal examinations.

The single-file climb up the stairs to the Great Hall was perhaps the most unnerving test of them all. As they ascended, doctors on both sides of the stairs would conduct a "six-second physical" on every immigrant. Was the immigrant breathing heavily? Was he or she limping? Did anyone have a physical problem that could make it hard to work? Once at the top of the stairs, they would walk in a circle in front of another doctor, who would examine the immigrant's hair and face.

The doctors were searching for any type of contagious disease, such as lice or *trachoma*. Immigrants not singled out for medical problems moved on; the others were marked with a piece of chalk. An "H" stood for heart disease, an "E" for eye problems, and an "X" for possible mental illness. Those with markings were *detained* for further examination. If their problems were curable, the immigrant would be cared for in the Ellis Island hospital building. Those who could not be cured were prevented from entering the country and sent back to Europe.

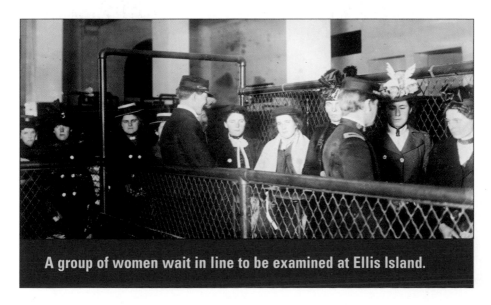

A group of women wait in line to be examined at Ellis Island.

The final step would be the legal examination. The immigrants would wait anxiously for their test with the other passengers from their ship. Every few minutes, the families would move, bench after bench, towards the large American flag hanging over the examination desks. There, the inspectors, called commissioners, would yell out "Next!" and beckon to the next immigrant.

The commissioners were like judges on a court bench. Within two

Immigrants are inspected and processed at Ellis Island. Doctors examined the weary immigrants to make sure they were healthy, and testers did their best to filter out criminals.

A GRANDMOTHER REMEMBERS ELLIS ISLAND

Lara Bisset emigrated from France in 1920 at the age of 10. When asked about her experiences, she said:

"I don't remember our passage, except that it was dull, lengthy, and I thought it would never end. You don't see anything but water. Finally, when word got out that we were approaching land, everybody ran outdoors on deck. We were packed like sardines, gazing with such excitement and wonderment. I saw the Statue of Liberty. It was so impressive, so majestic, so meaningful. Freedom! Opportunity!

"Then I remember getting off the boat like herds of cattle. Everybody was pushing out onto the ferry that took us to Ellis Island. Suddenly, the children were *segregated*, and the parents were segregated, and we couldn't understand this. Why were we in a different room than the adults?

"I remember hordes of people. I remember the darkness, the wooden benches, the poorly lit hall, the babies screaming, the children crying, adults crying. It was awful. It was a bad experience. And lines, such long lines, and such impatience.

"But we were all right. Our papers were in order. We stayed overnight, and my mother's brother picked us up in a Model-T Ford. And we got into this car and started for Wilmington, Delaware."

minutes, they would pepper the immigrant with about 30 quick questions: "What is your name?" "Where are you coming from?" "Where are you going?" "Do you have any relatives in the United States?" "Do you have any money?" "Do you have a criminal record?"

A customs official pins labels to the coats of a German immigrant family in Ellis Island's Registry Hall. Workers had a coded system to label immigrants who had diseases or were suspected of having health problems.

If the immigrant answered any of the questions improperly, he or she would be taken out of the line and detained.

After all the questions were asked, the commissioner would then decide the fate of every hopeful immigrant with the thwack of a rubber stamp—accepted, detained, or deported. If successful, the immigrant would receive a landing card and be permitted to enter the United

States. About one-third settled in the New York City area, while the rest bought rail tickets to other destinations throughout the country.

The process of inspection was nerve-wracking. Immigrants in large families risked being separated from the rest of their families if they could not pass the tests. The rapid-fire legal examination was especially frightening for immigrants who could not speak English. It was the prospect of being denied entry, however, that scared the new arrivals the most.

Though Ellis was the island of hope for most immigrants, for those unfortunate souls turned away from the golden door, it was the island of tears. During the most active period of immigration at Ellis Island, about 250,000 people were denied admission to the United States and sent home. The two main reasons for excluding immigrants were if a doctor discovered a contagious disease or if a legal inspector thought the immigrant would cause trouble. Relatively few immigrants were sent home, however. The vast majority of immigrants were set free to begin their new lives in America, usually within only a few short hours after arriving.

Ellis Island has great symbolic importance to millions of Americans. The island is also important because it welcomed one of America's great waves of immigration. And, it witnessed the beginning of a new era—one of changing American attitudes towards immigration. As people and politicians started to feel that America was becoming "more crowded" and "less American," restrictions on immigration began to appear. ✴

This 1921 cartoon shows Uncle Sam permitting immigrants to trickle into the United States. During the early 20th century, the U.S. government passed several laws intended to reduce the numbers of immigrants coming to America.

5 The Narrowing Gate

The Emergency Quota Act, passed by Congress in 1921, signaled the first great break in America's immigration tradition. Though restrictions on immigration to the United States were not new—people judged to be "undesirables" had long been denied—this new measure was the first to restrict healthy and able people. How did this come about? How did a nation that so strongly welcomed immigration suddenly try to slow it?

There was, in fact, nothing sudden about this decision. Frustration and concern about immigration had been growing since the 1880s. Part of this had to do with the huge increase in immigration taking place at the time. During the 1880s, the number of new arrivals began to reach record highs and did not slow down until World War I. Americans were beginning to feel that their country was "filling up." Indeed, by 1890, the American West was no longer empty and almost all of the United States had been settled.

It wasn't just the numbers that worried Americans, however, but rather the *type* of immigrants coming through the gate. With so many unfamiliar faces showing up on American streets, many people feared that the new immigrants would harm their society. For example, with the large-scale immigration of Roman Catholics and Jews from southern and eastern Europe, America was no longer a mostly Protestant country. Many also felt that these new immigrant groups were somehow inferior to those of the older waves of immigration. Fears about immigrants taking jobs from American-born citizens caused problems as well.

From the beginning of mass immigration through Ellis Island, there was increasing pressure on the government to place more restrictions on immigration into America. It was no longer enough that only convicts, the diseased, and *anarchists* be excluded. Many felt that it was now necessary to legally deny immigrants from certain countries and to limit the numbers coming in. The Chinese Exclusion Act of 1882 was the first major attempt at doing this.

In the 1850s, the Chinese had flocked to California to fulfill the demands for cheap labor as the territory expanded. Soon they numbered in the tens of thousands. The Chinese competed for jobs with other Americans. This sparked anti-Asian prejudice and led to anti-Chinese riots in San Francisco.

Politicians reacted with the introduction of the Chinese Exclusion Act, which banned Chinese immigration for a decade. Another 10-year

This colored postcard shows a Chinese family in America, circa 1900. Chinese Americans were resented for their industriousness and their cultural values

exclusion was imposed in 1892, and the ban was made permanent in 1902. It was not until 1965 that the restriction was abolished.

The Chinese were shunned in Canada as well. Concerned about the number of Chinese who came to build the Pacific Railway, Canadians wanted to make Chinese entry into Canada more difficult. In 1885, an act was passed to "restrict and regulate Chinese immigration." The act placed a large tax of $50 on every Chinese immigrant. This was later raised to $500, making it impossible for most Chinese to enter. Even stricter measures were imposed in 1923. Though Canada officially had an open door policy, like most Americans at the time Canadians also wanted only white British or Northern European immigrants allowed into their country.

Japanese Americans suffered even more. After Japan bombed Pearl Harbor in 1941, the government felt that Japanese Americans were a "security threat." Thousands of these immigrants, many of them already America citizens, were forced into detention or labor camps.

Other attempts restricting immigration to America followed. The Alien Contract Labor Law of 1885 prohibited Americans from importing contract labor, and the Literacy Act of 1917 ensured that only immigrants who could read and write would be allowed in. Each of these laws tried to slow immigration, but it soon became obvious that neither helped to slow the tide of new arrivals.

The demand for stricter anti-immigration laws continued after the end of World War I. Many Americans feared that millions of people from war-torn Europe were preparing to cross the Atlantic. There was also an increase in **xenophobia**, with a number of outwardly racist

THE NOT-SO-GOLDEN GATEWAY

Less known, but equally important for hundreds of thousands of immigrants, was the Ellis Island of the West—Angel Island Immigration Station. Located near the Golden Gate Bridge in San Francisco Bay, the station was the first stop for immigrants crossing the Pacific Ocean between 1910 and 1940. Though Chinese immigrants were the most common, Angel Island also processed many Japanese, Korean, Filipino, and Indian newcomers.

Like their European counterparts, Asian immigrants hoped to escape the economic and political hardships of their homelands. American society, however, was generally less accepting of Asians and less welcoming to them. A series of restrictive laws existed to keep Asians—particularly the Chinese—out of America. This was reflected in the conditions at Angel Island.

As they steamed into the harbor, the immigrants' first image of the station was a peaceful one: a quiet hillside dotted with palm trees and neat structures. As they got closer, however, locked gates, guard towers, and barbed wire fences began to paint a different picture. Angel Island was, in fact, more of a detention center than an immigrant-processing center.

books and articles appearing in the media and popular culture.

In response, Congress passed the Emergency Quota Act in 1921. The law set a limit of 357,000 immigrants per year and introduced quotas for eligible national groups. This resulted in a drastic reduction in the number of new immigrants. Next, the National Origins Act of 1924 laid down a permanent immigration policy. Not only did the Act reduce even further the number of immigrants to be allowed in each year (to 150,000), it introduced a quota system based on national origin. The system was an attempt to preserve the ethnic flavor of America's "old immigrant" society, and favored immigrants from northwestern Europe. Though it underwent a number of small changes, the National Origins Act remained the basis of American immigration policy until 1965.

The strict system was followed, and immigration fell sharply. The United States did make some important exceptions at times, however. Refugees were often allowed in under special conditions. Between 1933 and 1945, more than 160,000 European Jews fleeing Adolf Hitler's **anti-Semitic** policies were accepted. The United States also accepted 30,000 Hungarian refugees when the Soviet Union crushed their revolution in 1956, and 650,000 Cubans after Fidel Castro took power.

After World War II, attitudes about immigration and the national origins quota system began to change. President Harry Truman, who was an early champion of immigration reform, called the National Origins Act a "discriminatory policy" that was "utterly unworthy" of American traditions and ideals. Indeed, the law was not only unfair, it offended millions of Americans whose ancestors had come from the countries the law discriminated against.

Similar attitudes towards immigration were developing in Canada. The major turning point was the adoption of the Canadian Bill of Rights in 1960. For the first time in Canada's history, it was illegal to discriminate on the grounds of race, national origin, color, or religion. Canada's immigration laws changed significantly as a result.

The drive to **abolish** the National Origins Act succeeded in 1965 when President Lyndon Johnson signed the Immigrant and Nationality Act in a ceremony at the Statue of Liberty. The new bill promised that all immigrants applying for entry, regardless of national origin, race, creed, or color, would be treated equally. It did not, however, allow for any large increase in immigration. Only 170,000 people would be allowed to enter from the Eastern Hemisphere and 120,000 from the Western. Exceptions could be made, however, for relatives of individuals already in the United States and for refugees escaping political oppression or war.

This resulted in a huge change in the pattern of immigration to America. With thousands of Asian Americans inviting family members over, newcomers were more often from Asia than from Europe. The war in Vietnam and the spread of **Communism** also sent many Asians to America during the 1950s, 1960s, and 1970s. Most of the hundreds of thousands of refugees seeking **asylum** in America were Vietnamese, Chinese, Cambodians, and Laotians. Many Japanese, Filipinos, and Koreans also arrived.

Most immigrants after 1965 came from Mexico. Immigration from Mexico was already posing unique problems for American authorities.

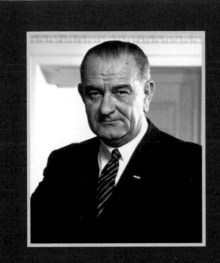

In 1965, President Lyndon B. Johnson signed the Immigration and Nationality Act into law. This legislation ended the quota system that favored immigrants from Western Europe. It gave people from all countries a chance to come to America.

Though many came legally, between 1924 and 1969 nearly six million Mexicans tried to sneak in illegally and were caught and deported. As demand for cheap labor increased in the 1970s, this problem became even worse. By 1980, nearly one million illegal Mexican migrants were being caught each year. Today, thousands come into America as legal immigrants, but many also attempt to make it over the border by illegal means.

The clauses allowing exceptions for family members and refugees has made the United States a major immigrant-accepting nation again. By the 1980s and 1990s, America was welcoming near-record numbers of immigrants—sometimes more than half a million new immigrants every year. ✳

Across the country every day, students recite the pledge of allegiance to the American flag. This convention began in the late 19th century, when Francis Bellamy penned the oath and began a campaign to make it a school tradition.

6 A Nation of Nations

The 2006 American Community Survey, a project of the U.S. Census Bureau, shows that America is more culturally diverse than ever before in its history. Together, the United States and Canada make North America the most diverse region on Earth. Nowhere else in the world and at no other time in history have so many cultures, races, and religions lived together for so long.

In the most recent U.S. Census, Elmhurst, a small city just outside of New York, was identified as the most culturally diverse zip code in the country. Since Elmhurst has been a popular destination for immigrants since the 1600s, it is an excellent example of the immigration experience. You only need to keep your ears open on Elmhurst's streets to see how American life has changed over the centuries. Two or three hundred years ago, the only language you heard was English, and maybe Dutch. Then you began to hear German. After that—Polish, Italian, and Yiddish. Then came Spanish. Today, you can hear Korean, Chinese, Vietnamese, Thai, Hindi, and even Punjabi among many others!

And just watching diversity in action shows that it can work. In overcrowded Newton High School—the most diverse school in America's most diverse zip code—there are 4,200 students. Born in 96 different countries, they speak 59 different languages. Nearly half of them are learning English as a second language.

The students adapt quickly, however. They learn English, begin each day by saluting the American flag and repeating the pledge of allegiance, and learn about American history and American heroes. By the time many of them graduate, it will be impossible to tell that they were not born in the United States. Slowly but surely, America becomes their home country.

However, America is not the "melting pot" it once was. In the early days of immigration, Americans simply assumed that people from all cultures would come to the United States and be absorbed into their culture. We can see in Elmhurst, however, that the ideal of the melting pot has disappeared. It is much more fitting to describe America today as a nation of nations.

Recent data from the U.S. Census Bureau indicates that this is an accurate description. Of the more than 303 million people in the United States, 44 million are Hispanic in origin, another 38 million are black or African American, 13.4 million are Asian, 2.9 million are Native Americans, and 20 million are of a variety of other races. More than 6 million people said that they draw their heritage from two or more races.

Population figures also show that the United States is still home to many new immigrants. Over 37 million people living in America today are foreign-born. Most of these immigrants come from Latin America, but large groups also come from Asia and Europe. Though some have been *naturalized* as American citizens, others have not.

Today, most Americans accept and support diversity. They believe that all Americans have the right to preserve their ethnic identity and still be a proud and loyal American citizen. While ethnic differences

In 2006, proposed changes to U.S. immigration policies sparked protests throughout the country. The bill—known in the House of Representatives as HR4437—would have required the government to jail undocumented immigrants. Congress ultimately did not pass HR4437.

can and do cause problems at times, there is still a strong sense of common purpose. Everywhere around the world, people are amazed at the ability of the United States to bring so many people from so many different backgrounds together.

In this way, history is repeating itself. When America's founding fathers were developing the country's government more than 200 years

THE MYTH OF THE MELTING POT

The idea of America as a "melting pot" of nations can be traced to the earliest days of statehood. In 1782, Frenchman Michel de Crèvecoeur observed that Americans were not simply transplanted Europeans, but a blend of different ethnic groups. He saw the United States as a place where "individuals of all nations are melted into a new race of men."

However, it wasn't until the early 1900s that the term "melting pot" came into use. It was the subject of a play by Israel Zangwill, an English Jew who had briefly visited America. The play's hero was a Jewish refugee fleeing his country for "waiting, beckoning, shining America." In the final scene, he praises his new home:

> America is God's Crucible, the great Melting Pot where all
> the races of Europe are melting and reforming—German and
> Frenchmen, Irishmen and Englishmen, Jews and Russians—
> into the Crucible with you all! God is making the American.

Though most critics were not impressed with the play when it opened, it touched at least one important audience member. Right after it finished, President Theodore Roosevelt shouted, "That's a great play, Mr. Zangwill!" across the theater to the author.

A section of a controversial wall being constructed along the U.S. border with Mexico, 2008. The wall is intended to prevent illegal border crossings and slow undocumented, or illegal, immigration from Mexico and Central America.

ago, they took inspiration from the Iroquois Indian Confederacy. This group of six Native American tribes followed a principle of "unity in diversity." The tribes kept their own separate identities but still bonded with the others in the name of progress and mutual protection. The founding fathers captured this principle in the motto that can be found on the great seal of the United States, *E Pluribus Unum*—"from many, one." ✸

Chronology

c. 1000 Vikings land at L'Anse aux Meadows, Newfoundland; archaeological evidence suggests that a temporary settlement was established there.

1492 Christopher Columbus makes landfall in the Bahamas; his voyage opens the great era of European exploration and colonization in the New World.

1565 The Spanish establish St. Augustine; it is the oldest continuously inhabited European settlement in North America.

1607 Jamestown, Virginia, is established as the first permanent English settlement in North America.

1619 The first African-American slaves arrive in Virginia.

1620 Pilgrims seeking religious freedom land in Massachusetts and establish the Plymouth colony.

1775–83 The American Revolution is fought; immigration comes to a virtual standstill.

1796 Introduction of the Land Purchase Act; under the act, immigrants could buy 320 acres at $2 an acre.

1815 End of the Napoleonic Wars in Europe; beginning of European migration to America on a massive scale.

1861–65 Immigration to the United States comes to a virtual halt during the American Civil War, a bloody conflict between the Northern and Southern states.

1862 Adoption of the Homestead Act, which granted 160 acres of public land to a settler after a five-year occupancy; the Act helped settle the West.

1882 Adoption of the Chinese Exclusion Act.

1886 Installation and dedication of the Statue of Liberty, a gift from France, in New York Harbor.

1892 Establishment of Ellis Island immigration station; by the time it closes in 1954, more than 12 million immigrants will be processed at the station.

1921 Congress passes the Emergency Quota Act; this law imposes numerical limits on immigrants for the first time.

1924 The National Origins Act becomes America's first permanent immigration policy, imposing further limits on immigration along with national quotas.

1939-45 World War II; thousands of Jews, among other Europeans, flee the war and are allowed entry to America as refugees.

1965 The Immigration and Nationality Act abolishes the quota system based on national origin; the new system still imposes numerical limits, but has many exemptions.

1980 The Refugee Act sets a limit on the number of refugees who will be admitted to the United States in a particular year.

1986 The Immigration Reform and Control Act makes it illegal for employers to hire immigrants who have not entered the country legally.

1990 The Immigration Act increases the number of legal immigrants permitted to enter the United States each year; Ellis Island is re-opened as a museum.

1996 Illegal Immigration Reform and Immigrant Responsibility Act sets easier standards for deportation.

2000 The U.S. census is held throughout the country, finding that the population of the United States is more than 281 million.

2001 The Child Citizenship Act, which gives citizenship to children born outside of the United States who have at least one citizen parent, goes into effect in February.

2003 The Immigration and Naturalization Service (INS) is dissolved; a new agency in the new Department of Homeland Security, Citizenship and Immigration Services, takes over most INS functions.

2005 The REAL ID Act permits the federal government to construct barriers at borders, and places more restrictions on immigrants.

2007 The population of the United States is estimated to be 303 million. The population of Canada is estimated at 33.4 million.

2008 Activists protest against the construction of a security fence along the U.S. border with Mexico.

Glossary

Abolish to end the observance or effect of.

Anarchist one who uses violent means to overthrow the existing order.

Anglicize to make or become English in pronunciation, habits, or customs.

Anti-Semitism prejudice, discrimination, or open hostility directed against Jews.

Artisan a craftsman or a person skilled in some industry or trade.

Asylum shelter, sanctuary.

Colonization the settlement of other territories by states.

Communism a system in which goods are owned in common and are available to all as needed.

Conscription compulsory enrollment of persons for military service.

Convoy a group that travels together for protection.

Detain to hold or keep in as if in custody.

Emigrate to leave one's own country for another.

Ethnic group a group of people with unique characteristics, customs, or languages.

Famine an extreme scarcity of food.

Indentured service people who were unable to afford an Atlantic passage could "borrow" the money, usually from a farmer. In return, they signed contracts, or "indentures," to work on the farm for a fixed number of years.

Migration the movement of a number of people to a new land.

Mosaic something made up of many different parts or elements.

Naturalization the process by which an immigrant officially becomes a citizen.

Oppression cruel or unfair treatment.

Persecution treating people badly, especially for religious, racial, or political reasons.

Plantation a large farm where crops like tobacco, cotton, sugar, coffee, or bananas are grown.

Pogrom an attack on minority groups.

Propaganda the spreading of ideas, information, or rumors for the purpose of helping or hurting an institution, a cause, or a person.

Segregate to separate or set apart from the general population.

Steerage the part of a passenger ship that is occupied by passengers traveling at the cheapest rate.

Trachoma a disease of the eye that causes blindness.

Xenophobia a hatred or fear of foreigners.

Further Reading

Bray, Ilona M., and Carl Falstrom. *U.S. Immigration Made Easy*. Berkeley, Calif.: NOLO, 2007.

Cieslik, Thomas, et al, editors. *Immigration: A Documentary and Reference Guide*. Westport, Conn.: Greenhaven Press, 2008.

Collier, C., and J.L. Collier. *A Century of Immigration, 1820–1924*. Tarrytown: Marshall Cavendish, 1999.

O'Donnell. *U.S. Immigration*. Mankato, Minn.: Capstone Press, 2008.

Schell, Richard, et al. *U.S. Immigration Citizenship Q&A*. Naperville, Ill.: Sphinx Publishing, 2008.

Tracing Your Immigrant Ancestors

Carmack, Sharon DeBartolo. *A Genealogist's Guide to Discovering Your Immigrant and Ethnic Ancestors: How to Find and Record Your Unique Heritage*. Cincinnati: Betterway Books, 2000.

Newman, John J. *American Naturalization Processes and Procedures, 1790–1985*. Bountiful, Utah: Heritage Quest, 1998.

Schaefer, Christina K. *Instant Information on the Internet! A Genealogist's No-Frills Guide to the Fifty States and the District of Columbia*. Baltimore: Genealogical Publishing Co., 1999.

Szucs, Loretto Dennis, and Sandra Hargreaves, editors. *The Source: A Guidebook of American Genealogy*. Salt Lake City: Ancestry Inc., 1997.

Taylor, Maureen. *Uncovering Your Ancestry Through Family Photographs*. Cincinnati: Betterway Books, 1999.

Internet Resources

http://www.census.gov

The official Web site of the U.S. Bureau of the Census contains information about the most recent census taken in 2000.

http://www.uscis.gov/portal/site/uscis

The U.S. Citizenship and Immigration Service's official Web site provides information on how to become a citizen, as well as the rights and responsibilities of citizenship.

http://www.ellisisland.org/

This Web site is devoted to the history of Ellis Island and the immigrants who came through its doors.

http://www.angelisland.org/

The official Web site for the Angel Island Immigration Station Foundation. Angel Island was an immigration and quarantine station for nearly 100 years, and is now a state park.

http://www.statueofliberty.org

This Web site is dedicated to the history, preservation and restoration of the Statue of Liberty.

http://www.archives.gov/index.html

This is the National Archives and Records Administration Web site, providing a place where people can conduct research on family members who came to America.

Index

Numbers in ***bold italic*** refer to captions

Photo Credits

Contributors

Barry Moreno has been librarian and historian at the Ellis Island Immigration Museum and the Statue of Liberty National Monument since 1988. He is the author of *The Statue of Liberty Encyclopedia*, which was published by Simon & Schuster in October 2000. He is a native of Los Angeles, California. After graduation from California State University at Los Angeles, where he earned a degree in history, he joined the National Park Service as a seasonal park ranger at the Statue of Liberty; he eventually became the monument's librarian. In his spare time, Barry enjoys reading, writing, and studying foreign languages and grammar. His biography has been included in *Who's Who Among Hispanic Americans, The Directory of National Park Service Historians, Who's Who in America,* and *The Directory of American Scholars*.

Peter Hammerschmidt runs his freelance writing and editing service through Wordschmidt Communications. A policy analyst for the federal government of Canada, he lives in Ottawa.